Puzzling Mazes

LEE DANIEL QUINN

DOVER PUBLICATIONS, INC.
New York

To my three grandchildren:

Michael, Alyssa and Zoe.
From Gramps

Bibliographical Note

Puzzling Mazes is a new work, first published by Dover Publications, Inc., in 1994.

International Standard Book Number: 0-486-27980-4

Manufactured in the United States of America
Dover Publications, Inc., 31 East 2nd Street,
Mineola, N.Y. 11501

Introduction

When you were younger, I'm sure you found fun in doing simple mazes. You might be interested to know that the maze is a very, very old form of art. Mazes were to be found in ancient caves, in Egypt in biblical times, and in England during the time of Robin Hood and his Merry Men. One of the most famous mazes has been traced to Crete, an island in the Mediterranean Sea. There was a special maze there which contained a ferocious bull. Prisoners were sent into the maze and most never returned. In England, there is a Tudor palace called Hampton Court that dates back to the year 1514. On the grounds of this estate is a maze made up of hedges that visitors still enjoy walking through.

The mazes in this book are, I hope, more challenging than most puzzles you have done in the past. The book has the easier mazes in the front, working up to the tougher ones later on. You will find, under the title of each maze, an indication (easy, medium or difficult) of how hard the maze is to solve. You should always read the page opposite the puzzle. You will find important information about the maze there. There is one rule that applies to all the mazes you find in the book: unless you are told differently, you may never go over the same path twice.

There are several kinds of mazes in this book. The first, and most familiar, is the flat maze. If you have done any mazes, this is the kind of puzzle you are familiar with. The second kind of maze is the under-and-over paths. When you come to the first under-and-over, I have included a diagram to explain them. You will also find that some mazes ask you to follow special instructions that appear on the page opposite the puzzle. I sincerely hope you enjoy this book of *Puzzling Mazes*. If you like this one, I will certainly produce another for your enjoyment!

LEE DANIEL QUINN
Middlesex County

Through the Gate

EASY

As you can see, there is a wide gate in the center of this maze.

You must first find your way from the top opening to the center gate.

Your next job is to choose the correct path from the center gate through the bottom opening.

Arrow One

EASY

I call this puzzle "Arrow One" because I want to show you another kind of maze.

When you look at the paths, they all seem to be open. This is not so.

The rule is that you must always go along a path the way the arrow points. As soon as you meet an arrow going the opposite way you are traveling, you must stop and go back.

With this rule in mind, you must start at the top opening and you win when you get through the exit at the bottom.

Egyptian Halls

Ancient civilizations all over the world used mazes in their religion and their art. Some gardeners even made their garden hedges into mazes.

When you go on to study ancient history, I'm sure you will be surprised to find the many places that mazes turn up.

In some of the temples I visited in Egypt, I found that the builders seemed to like long rectangular halls when they were building for the Pharaoh.

This puzzle, with its long passages, reminded me of those temples.

When you find your way to the bottom, you will have solved the mystery of the Egyptian Halls.

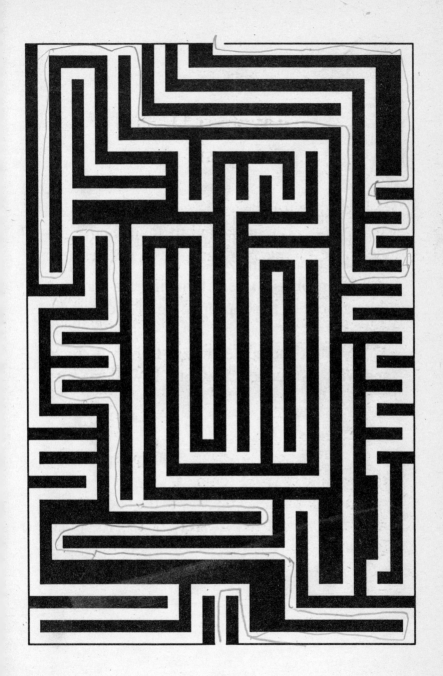

Rat Maze

Well, Robert B. Rat is in trouble this time!

He finds himself in the center of Professor Mazzle's meanest maze.

Your job is to help him find his way out through either the top opening or the bottom one.

Start at the center where Robert is stuck and with your pencil show him how to get out.

It's Your Choice

Here's one you can't lose. You have two choices, Happy or Sad. It's up to you!

Start at the top of the puzzle, keep picking one path or the other, and you are sure to wind up with one face or the other.

To give it a certain suspense, you should tell yourself which of the two faces you are heading for before you start on your journey.

Mario's Computer

EASY

When Mario comes home at night, he likes to play games on his computer.

The only problem is that to play with his computer, he must first turn it on.

Like everything in Mario's life, his task is not an easy one!

As you can see, he must get to the on–off switch at the bottom before he can enjoy himself.

You can help by drawing a line from the top to the switch at the bottom.

OFF ON

Put Out That Fire!

EASY

When the fire alarm rings, every second counts! When the firemen hear the bell, they slide down the pole, jump into their fire engines, and race to the fire.

When they get to the fire, they look for the nearest fire hydrant and connect their hoses to it.

When they turn on the hydrant, the water rushes through the hose and the firemen spray the fire with lots of water to put it out.

As a fireman, your important job is to bring the hose from the hydrant at the top of this maze, to the fire that is burning at the bottom.

Every moment counts, so please hurry!

Pipe Path #1

If you have ever seen pipes in your basement, you know that some pipes go behind others and some go in front.

In this puzzle, some of the paths go under others, and some go over.

Your job is to go from the top to the bottom. Before you try it, look at the example below.

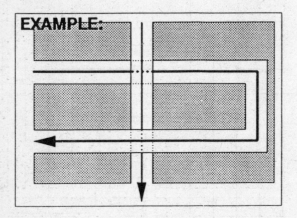

EXAMPLE:

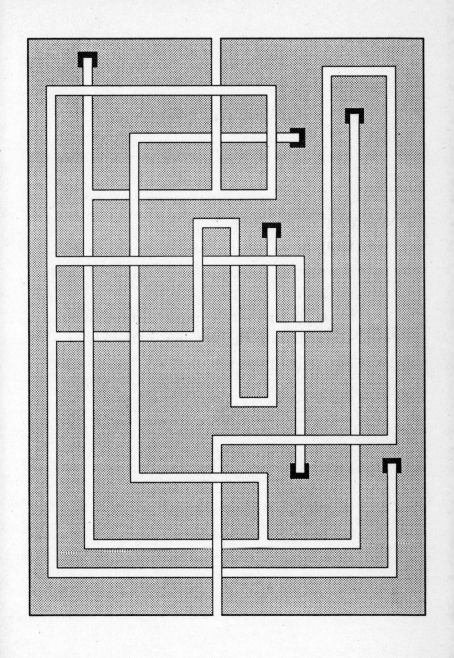

21

Down the Drain

EASY

Did you ever wonder where the water goes when you pull the plug?

Well, here's what I think happens to it!

Starting at the top—in the sink—follow the arrows down the drain.

Now, go through the pipes just like water, until you pour out the bottom into the sewer.

The only things you must watch out for are the clogs in the pipe. You can't get by them. They look like this: ✳

Don't forget to dry your hands.

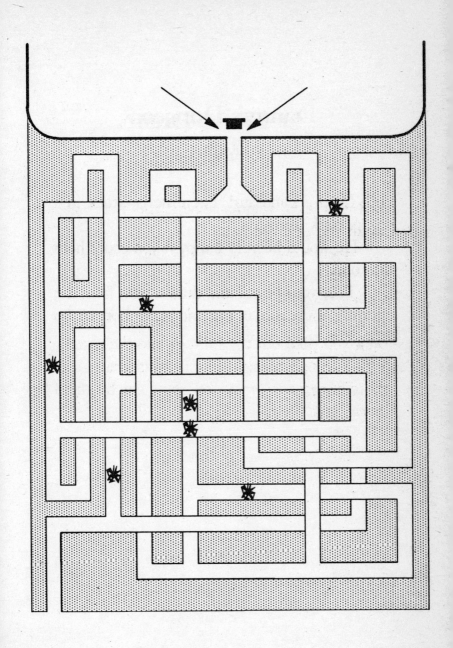

23

Danny's Dungeon

EASY

Poor Danny Dinosaur! There he is, stuck in a damp, dark dungeon.

He would be very happy if you could help him out.

Take your pencil and draw a path from the opening at the top, or the one at the bottom, to show him the easy way out.

Here's Looking at You

Just look at all those eyes staring up at you!

You are expected to start at the top and work your way down to the bottom.

Keep your eye out for those false paths!

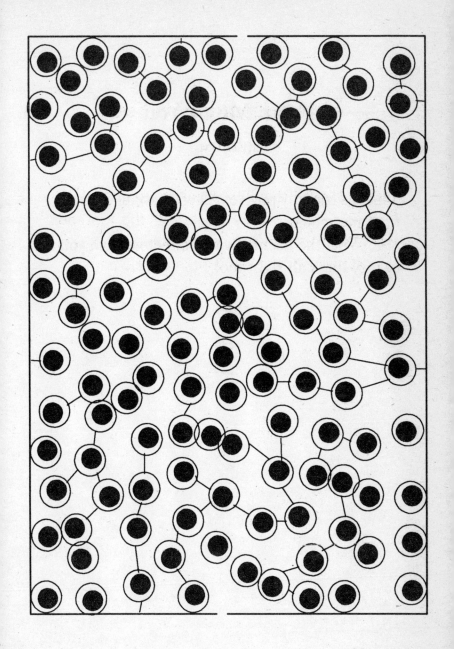

27

From Me to You

MEDIUM

This is a friendly puzzle. All you have to do is go from me to you.

What the heck! If you'd rather go from you to me, that's all right too!

Mirror Image

MEDIUM

If you look at this puzzle, you will see that it is in two parts—one above, and the other below.

They look *almost* the same, too. But that is where the puzzle is.

Each of the two parts is slightly different. The paths end and start in different places. So, after you find your way through the top half, don't count on using the same paths in the second part.

Like most of these puzzles, you start at the top and win when you come out at the bottom.

Boxes and Bars

MEDIUM

I guess you can see why I call this puzzle "Boxes and Bars"!

With all those nice gray boxes and black bars, it makes an interesting maze.

As usual, you are asked to start at the top opening and work your way down to the bottom.

Those black bars have a way of linking that makes this puzzle a bit harder than you would think at first.

At least I've given you some nice open spaces where you can rest and catch your breath.

33

"V" for Victory

MEDIUM

During World War II, Winston Churchill, the Prime Minister of England, would hold up his two fingers to form a "V" for victory. England was losing the war and he wanted to cheer everybody up by reminding them that victory was possible.

You will be victorious in solving this puzzle if you keep your courage and do your best.

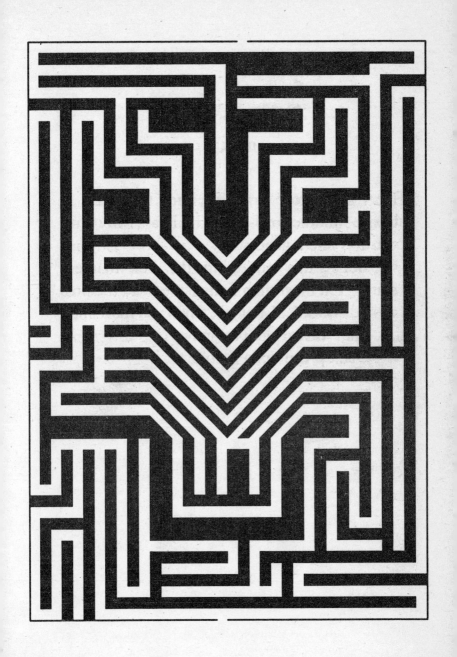

A Good Story

MEDIUM

Every good story has three important parts: a start, a middle and an end. That's why this puzzle is like a good story.

Begin this puzzle in the box marked "start." You must then find your way to the box marked "middle." You win when you move into the "end" box at the bottom.

OK: "Once upon a time . . ."

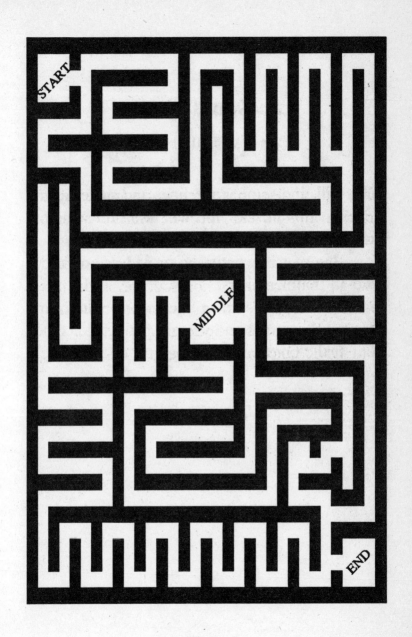

Lines and Curves

You will find some smile lines and some frown lines in this puzzle. You will also find some of the same curves in a side view.

No matter what they remind you of, they are all troublemakers.

You are to start at the top opening, zip around the curves and straight paths, and come out at the bottom with a big grin on your face.

39

Chevrons

MEDIUM

The stripes that an army sergeant wears on his arm are called chevrons.

When I made up this puzzle, I could see those chevrons over and over again.

Like most of the other mazes, you should start at the top and you win when you leave at the bottom.

So, start up and pay *attention*!

41

Here's Looking, Again

MEDIUM

I hate to tell you this, but there seems to be someone looking at you in the maze on the opposite page.

He seems to be daring you to cross his face and tickle his chin as you find your way from the top to the bottom of this interesting puzzle.

Which is the Wall?

This is a strange problem, indeed! In every other maze, you follow the white path and, if it is the right one, you come out the bottom as a winner.

In this puzzle, the winning path can be either the white one or the gray one. That's why I ask, "Which is the wall?"

Start at any one of the arrows at the top (there are four of them), and come out at one of the arrows at the bottom.

There is only one winner—is it gray or white? That's for you to find out!

As Simple as A-B-C

MEDIUM

How many times have you heard someone say, "It's as simple as A-B-C"? Plenty, I'll bet.

Well, here you have A, B, C and D. All you have to do is connect just *two* of the four letters shown. Isn't that easy?

Start at any of the four corners, that is, either A, B, C or D, and then follow the trail until it comes to any other letter.

Remember: only two of the letters connect!

I'd like to give you a hint but that would make it as simple as A-B-C.

Fill 'Er Up!

MEDIUM

The whole family is going on a trip to Disneyland. But, when dad looks at the gas gauge, he sees that the tank is almost empty.

If you want to get on your way, you will have to go to the gas station and fill 'er up.

You are handed the map and asked to draw a line to the gas pump.

Start at the car at the top and find your way to the gas pump at the bottom.

Remember, you can't go the wrong way on a one-way street. The arrows show you which streets are one-way, and which way you must go.

This is an under-and-over puzzle and you may go under streets as the map shows.

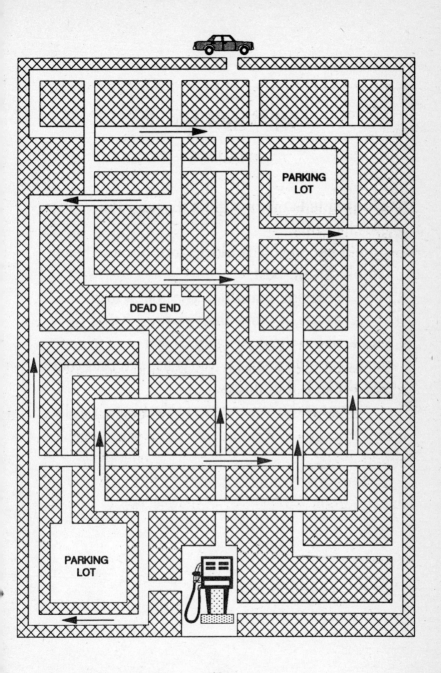

Big Black Blocks

MEDIUM

This reminds me of a great tongue twister that goes like this:

"I like big black blocks lots, because black big blocks are best."

Try saying that three times in a row!

Anyway, it looks like your kid brother left his blocks on the floor again. If you want to go to the kitchen for a snack, you'll have to find your way through the blocks.

Start at the top and get to the kitchen at the bottom.

KITCHEN

The Club House

MEDIUM

Charlie Brown has called an important meeting at the club house! So, starting at the top, find your way to the meeting.

No matter which way you go, you are sure to wind up at the club house in the center of this puzzle.

After you have your meeting, you must make your way out the bottom.

You may find that the way out is a lot harder to find than the way in, so keep trying until you get it right!

Decisions . . . Decisions!

MEDIUM

As soon as you enter this puzzle at the top, you meet arrows indicating two paths you may follow.

Like most things in everyday life, there are always two sides to every story.

In this puzzle, you will see 14 places where you must make a decision.

If you make all the right decisions, you will be able to exit from the bottom.

Oh! If you make a wrong turn, I've put a gray pillow for you to bump into.

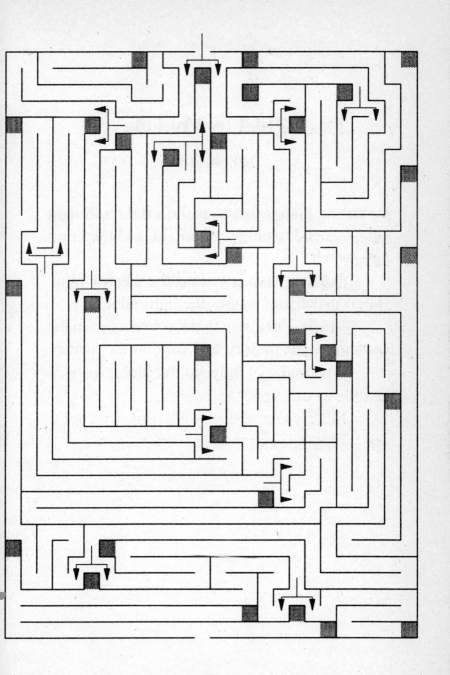

Light Up My Life

DIFFICULT

Everyone knows that to make a lightbulb light up, you need to plug the lamp in, and then turn the switch.

Your first task is to find the electric plug. Then make your way to the lightbulb.

Finally, I'm going to ask you to move to the bottom of the puzzle, and turn on the switch.

Go ahead . . . light up my life!

One Gold Star

DIFFICULT

Do you remember, back in kindergarten, when the teacher gave you a gold star if you did good work?

Well, this next puzzle has stars, but unfortunately they are not gold.

You start at the top of the puzzle and work your way down to the bottom counting stars you pass.

You earn a star when you pass over it on your way through the maze.

IMPORTANT! No one likes a show-off so you may not pass more than one star. If you pass more than one star you must start over again.

59

End of the Rainbow

DIFFICULT

Everyone knows that there is a pot of gold at the end of the rainbow.

Here we have four rainbows, one in each corner of the puzzle.

Your job is to find out which path leads to the pot of gold sitting right in the middle of the puzzle.

Start at any one of the four rainbows and try that path. If it isn't the right one, start at another.

Everyone will find the right path within three tries. See if you can find the correct path on the first try!

61

Get Going!!!

DIFFICULT

The fire alarm sounds. Drop what you are doing and get out of the maze!

Starting in the center, you have two ways to escape: from the bottom or out the top. It is up to you.

Remember, walk—don't run—to the nearest exit.

On the Square

DIFFICULT

In the olden days, when you said that someone was "on the square," you meant that he was honest and could be trusted.

I'm afraid that, with this puzzle, you can't trust your eyes.

But, you can be sure that there really is one path from the top to the bottom.

Trust me on this!

Counting Out

In this puzzle, it doesn't matter if you go 1-2-3 or 3-2-1. But you must decide which to come out a winner.

Start from the top opening, then go to either 3 or 1. Then go to the next number, which must be 2. Then go to 1 or 3, depending whether you are going up (1-2-3) or down (3-2-1).

Finally, make your way out through the bottom to be a winner.

Simple as 1-2-3.

Swat That Fly!

DIFFICULT

Here's an easy job for you. Mom asks you to get the fly swatter and swat that fly.

Well, maybe it's not too easy! The first problem is to pick the right door to enter. As you can see, there is one door at the top and another one at the bottom.

I'll bet you can guess that only one door is the right one.

First, you must get the fly swatter. Then you must find your way to the fly to swat it.

This puzzle is as hard as swatting flies with a pencil. So look sharp and get to work.

Shaky Spider

Sam the shaky spider is stuck in the middle of his own web!

Somehow, he has to find openings in his web that will let him get out of the mess he is in.

Starting from the center, you must find the right set of gaps in his web to let him escape by the bottom or the top.

He's counting on you!

Add 'Em Up

DIFFICULT

This looks like a simple adding problem, but you will find it harder than it looks.

Starting from the top, make your way to any one of the small number blocks.

Remember that number and go back into the puzzle. You can then go on to another number, or head for one of the three bottom answers.

You win when you can match the total of the numbers you find to the answer.

For example, if you went through the "2" box and the "1" box, you win when you find your way to the "=3" at the bottom.

If you only went through a "2" box, you win if you can get to the "=2" at the bottom.

Finally, if you went through each of the "2" boxes, you win if you get to the "=4" box at the bottom.

Such small numbers can still be quite puzzling.

Transporter Madness

DIFFICULT

The captain wants to put a team down on planet Teragram to explore the planet. Your job is to enter at the top and pick the right transporter.

As you can see, there are three transporters. They are programmed to beam you down to one of three spots on the planet.

Only one of the planet transporter receivers will let you complete your mission by leaving by the bottom port.

So pick your transporter carefully or you will have to go back to the spaceship and try to find another.

Don't worry, the natives are friendly and the air is breathable!

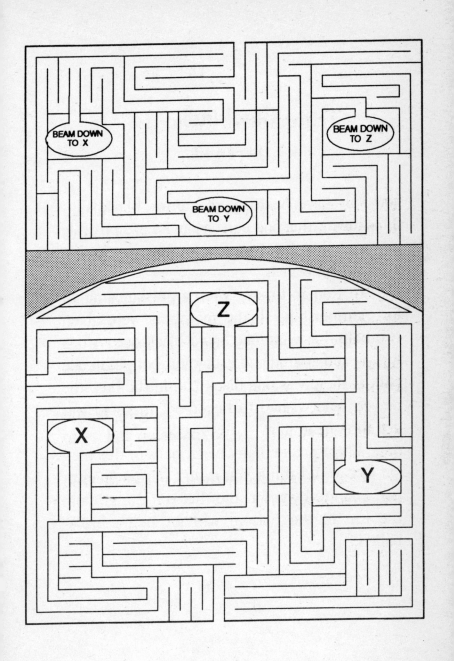

75

Blackball

You may have heard of the term "blackball." This means that one person can keep a possible new member from joining a group by voting against him or her.

In Roman times, when a person came up for membership, all the members were given two balls—a white one and a black one. A box was passed around and each member put in one ball. If there was one black ball in the box, the person who wished to become a member was not allowed to join.

There are so many black balls in this puzzle you would think you didn't have a chance. But I can tell you for sure that you can go from the top to the bottom without being blackballed!

One-Way Streets

DIFFICULT

If you look carefully, you will see that most of
the paths go through from the top to the bottom.

What makes this a puzzle is the arrows that
are in some of the paths.

The rule is that you may not pass an arrow
that is pointing the opposite way from the way
you are going.

Follow the right one-way streets and you
will find your way through this maze.

79

Wormhole!

This is really a spaced-out wormhole. The direction you must take is indicated either with one- or two-headed arrows. You must always go the way the arrow points. When you find a two-headed arrow you can go either way.

This is the only puzzle where you can go over the same path twice.

Start at the top opening, then go right to the wormhole in the center. Next, find your way out through the bottom opening.

Ensign, set a course for the bottom. Course laid in? OK, engage!

Three Ends

DIFFICULT

Start where it says "start," and go to any of the three ends. Yes, that's what I said—go to any one of the three end boxes that are in the corners of the puzzle.

How easy can you get? I'm not asking you to pick out one particular finishing spot, you can choose *any one*.

Well, maybe it isn't as easy as it looks. It could be that you can get to only one of the ends. I said *maybe*. You will have to find out for yourself.

83

A Bad Dream

DIFFICULT

Well, that's what it looks like to me! You start this dream at the top and zigzag through the many sharp points until you pop out at the bottom (without any scars, I hope!).

85

SOLUTIONS

Through the Gate, page 6

Arrow One, page 8

Egyptian Halls, page 10

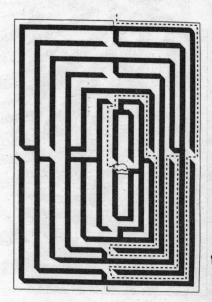

Rat Maze, page 12

It's Your Choice, page 14

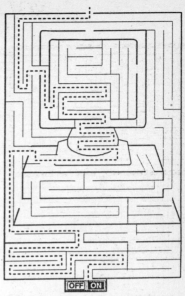

Mario's Computer, page 16

Put Out That Fire!, page 18

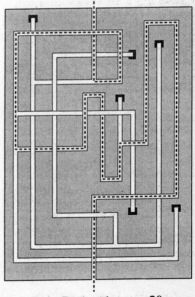

Pipe Path #1, page 20

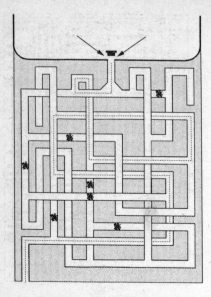

Down the Drain, page 22

Danny's Dungeon, page 24

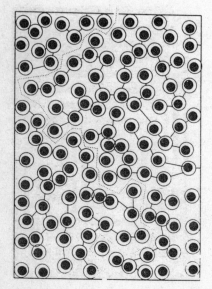

Here's Looking at You, page 26

From Me to You, page 28

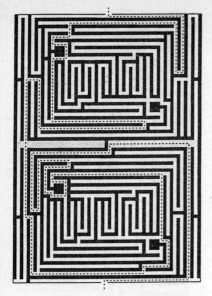

Mirror Image, page 30

Boxes and Bars, page 32

"V" for Victory, page 34

A Good Story, page 36

Lines and Curves, page 38

Chevrons, page 40

Here's Looking, Again, page 42

Which Is the Wall?, page 44

90

As Simple as A-B-C, page 46

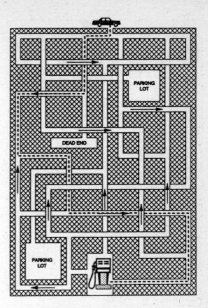

Fill 'Er Up!, page 48

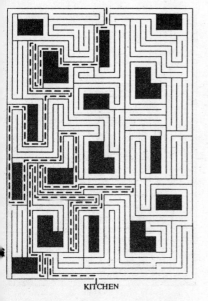

Big Black Blocks, page 50

The Club House, page 52

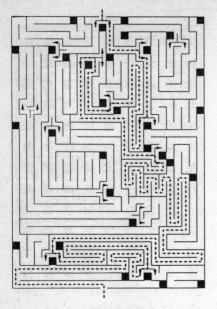

Decisions . . . Decisions!, page 54

Light Up My Life, page 56

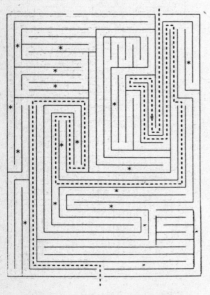

One Gold Star, page 58

End of the Rainbow, page 60

Get Going!!!, page 62

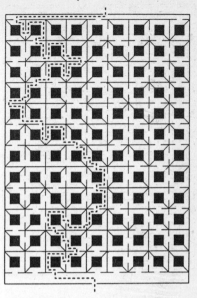

On the Square, page 64

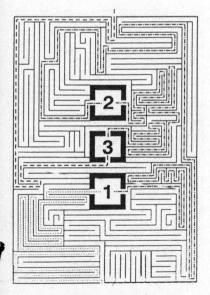

Counting Out, page 66

Swat That Fly!, page 68

Shaky Spider, page 70

Add 'Em Up, page 72

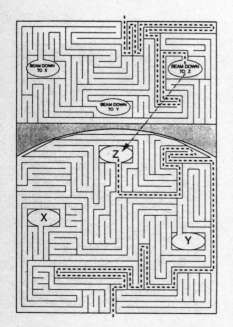

Transporter Madness, page 74

Blackball, page 76

One-Way Streets, page 78

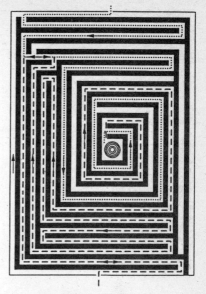

Wormhole!, page 80

Three Ends, page 82

A Bad Dream, page 84